# Parables from the Animal Kingdom

by John Calvin Reid,

illustrated by Bryan Stone

STANDARD PUBLISHING
Cincinnati, Ohio        24-02872

Edited by Theresa Hayes

**LIBRARY OF CONGRESS**
**Library of Congress Cataloging-in-Publication Data**

Reid, John Calvin, 1901-

    Parables from the animal kingdom/by John Calvin Reid.
       p.    cm.

    Summary: Twelve parables in which animal characters with human traits encounter and resolve problems such as prejudice, peer pressure, pride, disobedience, and selfishness, and come to appreciate good traits such as bravery, kindness, hope, and generosity.

    ISBN 0-87403-500-7: $4.95 (est.)
    1. Kingdom of God—Juvenile literature. [1. Parables. 2. Christian life. 3. Conduct of life.] I. Title.
BT94.R33 1988                           87-32922
241'.4—dc19                                CIP
                                               AC

# DEDICATION

*To all lovers of God's creatures,*
  *Large and small,*
*And to the great God who made them;*
  *Lord over all.*

# Contents

# INTRODUCTION

What is a parable?

The dictionary defines it as "a short fictitious story from which a moral or spiritual truth is drawn." But I much prefer the definition of the little child, "an earthly story with a heavenly meaning."

The stories in this book have been written with this simple but profound definition always in mind. That is why I call them "parables."

It is my hope that children will not only find pleasure in reading these stories, but will enjoy still more seeking out the "heavenly meanings" which lie, partly hidden and partly revealed, in each.

A prayer has been added at the end of each parable to help children apply the lesson the parable teaches.

It is my further hope that pastors, teachers, and parents will also find the stories useful and effective in teaching children the basic truths of Christian character. To further assist them in this worthy endeavor, a selection of supportive Bible references and appropriate poems has been provided as an appendix to each parable.

—The Author

# The Parable of
# The Prejudiced Birds

*I do not know why the skin of some people is black, of others white, why some have brown skin, and others, yellow. But I think I do know why the blood of every person in the world is red. This is God's way of telling us that we are all alike "inside." He wants us to know and to remember that all of us are His children; "under the skin," blood brothers and sisters!*

*Here is a story of how the birds were once taught this lesson, in a way they could never forget!*

\* \* \* \* \*

What more beautiful creatures can you find in all the world than birds? Beautiful not only to look at, but also to listen to—what sweet songs they sing! And how nice it is that, for the most part, they all live together in harmony and peace!

But according to Mrs. Owl, who claims to know everything that ever happened in the forest, there was a war between the birds many years ago. Not a *shooting* war, for the birds had no guns, but a *plucking* war, for all the birds did have feathers, and sharp beaks to pluck the feathers with!

According to Mrs. Owl, it was Sleazy the Snake who caused all the trouble. Sleazy seemed to enjoy creating problems everywhere he went! It was one of his ancestors, according to Mrs. Owl, who was the cause of the trouble in the Garden of Eden years and years ago!

One day, Sleazy slithered over to where the redbirds were and said, "You know, *you* have the most beautiful feathers of all the birds in the forest! They are red like a glorious rose. But did you hear that the bluebirds say their feathers are prettier than yours?"

He then crawled over to the bluebirds and said, "What lovely feathers you have! They are the most beautiful of all the birds in the forest! They are blue like the heavenly sky. But have you heard that the redbirds say their feathers are prettier than yours?"

Sleazy whispered similar words into the ears of the beautiful, yellow-feathered canaries, and into the ears of the swans and the egrets, whose feathers were white. And into the ears of the sparrows, whose feathers were brown. And into the ears of the crows, whose feathers were black. And into the ears of other birds, whose feathers were mixed in color, such as the woodpeckers, the robins, and the painted buntings.

Now up to this time, according to Mrs. Owl, the birds had lived together in the great forest with very little thought given to the fact that their feathers were different in color. There was plenty of room for all and plenty of food for all, so the various birds built their nests, laid their eggs, and hatched their chicks with a warm, friendly feeling toward all other birds. Now and then, two might quarrel over a bug or a worm, but not for long. Peace and joy and song reigned day after day in Birdland.

But now, as Sleazy whispered his evil lies into the ears of all the birds, they began to be more and more color-conscious and unfriendly toward one another.

10

Finally one day, a redbird hopped over to a bluebird and plucked a feather out of his wing—not because he hated the bluebird, but just because he didn't like blue! And the angry bluebird plucked back, pulling a feather out of the redbird's wing!

The plucking spread, like a forest fire, until all the birds were at it, and feathers of all colors and sizes were floating here and there, then drifting to the ground like falling leaves! The plucking was really fast and furious—almost like a war! The birds screeched at one another as they plucked, and screamed in pain as they were plucked in return. All over the great forest, the battle raged and feathers flew. Only the darkness of night brought an end to the plucking,

and by that time, almost every bird in the forest had been stripped bare.

As the cold night air chilled their bodies, tempers cooled, and families of birds huddled together trying in vain to keep warm. Thoughts of their foolish behavior began to nag at them, but not until the next day dawned did they realize how very foolish they had been. Then, as the birds looked at each other in the morning light, they found to their amazement that stripped of their feathers, they all looked almost exactly alike! Not one could claim to be prettier than another; all were equally ugly! Worse still, to their great shame, with their feathers all gone, not one of them could fly! All were earthbound. They could only walk and hop! As for singing, some of them had strained their voices by shrieking, others had caught cold in the night, and all were so ashamed, that in the entire forest not one song was heard! What a sad, gloomy day it was in Birdland! A few never did recover their voices. To this day, for example, when the crow tries to sing, all that comes out is, "Caw, caw, caw!"

But the birds were sorry, and apologized to each other, and asked God to forgive them. In time, their feathers grew back, and once again they were able to spread their wings and soar upward toward the sky. Soon after, the great forest was filled once more with joyful song.

Best of all, there has never been another war between the birds! You see, they learned their lesson, and, year by year ever since, parent birds have taught that lesson to their chicks. The lesson the birds learned and still remember is this, "All colors are given by God, and in His sight, no color is ugly, but all are equally beautiful!"

# Prayer

*Dear Father God,*
*There are many boys and girls in all parts of the world, with skin of many different colors. We know You love them all and all are Your children. That makes all of them our brothers and sisters. Help us to remember that and to love them all, as You do. Amen.*

## What Does the Bible Say ...
# About Prejudice?

1 Samuel 16:7
Amos 9:7
Malachi 2:10
Luke 10:25-37 (especially 33)
John 4:1-26 (especially 9, 23)
Acts 8:26-38 (especially 27)
Acts 10:19-35 (especially 28, 34, 35)
Galatians 3:28
Colossians 3:11
Revelations 7:9

# More to Think About

## Who Is So Low?

Who is so low that I am not his brother?
Who is so high that I've no path to him?
Who is so poor I may not feel his hunger?
Who is so rich I may not pity him?
May none, then, call on me for understanding,
May none, then, turn to me for help in pain,
And drain alone his bitter cup of sorrow,
Or find he knocks upon my heart in vain.

Harlow

# No East Or West

In Christ there is no east or west,
   In Him no south or north;
But one great fellowship of love
   Throughout the whole wide earth.

Join hands, then, brothers of the faith,
   Whate'er your race may be:
Who serves my Father as a son
   Is surely kin to me.

In Christ now meet both east and west,
   In Him meet south and north:
All Christly souls are one in Him,
   Throughout the whole wide earth.

John Oxenham

# O Brother Man

O brother man, fold to thy heart thy brother;
Where pity dwells, the peace of God is there;
To worship rightly is to love each other,
Each smile is a hymn, each kindly deed a
   prayer.

Whittier

# The Parable of
# The Brave
# Roadrunner

*Many years ago, when the first citizens of the United States were moving from east to west, the land was very difficult to cross. It was a wilderness, full of mountains and swamps. There were no roads or bridges, no farms or factories, no mines or electricity, no towns or cities. Many brave men and women worked long and hard to settle the land, and it is important that we remember the price they paid—some of them paid with their lives—to make the United States the country that it is today!*

*In the story that follows, you will meet one of these pioneers—a Roadrunner, whose real name is chaparral.* Our story begins in the land of Mexico, many years ago.

✻ ✻ ✻ ✻ ✻

One evening, Paisano Chaparral and a number of other birds attended an illustrated lecture by the world-famous scout, Baldy Eagle. Baldy had just come back from a flight to North America, during which he had explored the Rio Grande river valley all the way to the Rocky Mountains of Colorado.

"Beautiful new country," he said, as he showed his Audubon picture slides, "but food is hard to find. Only a few song birds have moved in yet; it's too dangerous. Scorpions and snakes are everywhere! No nest is safe." Then he added, "If we could only find a few brave birds to go in as pioneers!"

At that point, Paisano lifted his wing and fluttered it back and forth. "You have a question?" Baldy asked.

"Yes, please, what is a pioneer?"

Baldy explained that a pioneer is someone who is willing to go first into a new country, open it up, and make it safe for others to follow.

Later that night, sitting beside a catus bush under a moonlit sky, Paisano said to himself, "I can't sing like the orioles, mockingbirds, and warblers, and my feathers are not beautiful like those of the bluebirds, cardinals, and painted buntings, but I do have strong legs and a sharp bill. Instead of taking it easy down here in Mexico, I could move up to that new country and clear out some of those scorpions and snakes to make it safe for the songbirds to come in."

And that is exactly what he did!

In those early days there were human pioneers too—men and women who opened new roads through the wilderness and drove their wagons through. As these humans saw Paisano running along in front of them, they were amazed at how fast he could move on such short legs, and began calling him "roadrunner." The name stuck. From that time on, "roadrunner" has been the chaparral's nickname!

But Paisano found other things to do besides running in front of the wagons. When the settlers and their horses were resting, Paisano would dart out into the fields in search of

18

lizards, scorpions, and snakes. Because the lizards always tried to run away, they were fairly easy to catch, but scorpions and snakes were fighters.

The first time he saw a scorpion lying on the top of a log, Paisano whispered to himself, "I know his tail is full of poison, and that sharp point on the end is his stinger. I must be quick and careful."

Then with one quick jump, he had the scorpion by the tail, and holding him tight in his bill, he pounded him up and down on the log. Never again would that scorpion be found stealing eggs from Mrs. Meadowlark's nest! Instead, he became a "Delicious Scorpion a la Chaparral," for Paisano's lunch. Paisano enjoyed every bite. Then, before moving on, he arranged the scorpion's stinger and claws in a neat little pile on top of the log to warn other scorpions to stay away from bird nests!

A few days later, Paisano met the most dreaded enemy of the birds, the rattlesnake. Mr. Rattler did not notice Paisano at first, because he had his evil eye fixed upon two little whippoorwills who stood frozen with fear as their hungry enemy slithered closer and closer.

"I've got to save them!" Paisano cried.

With a loud squawk, he swooped in. The little whippoorwills, no longer under the spell of Mr. Rattler's evil eye, hurried away into the bushes, while the rattlesnake, angry at being robbed of his dinner, turned upon Paisano.

"You cocky little rooster," he hissed. "I'll have chaparral for my dinner instead of whippoorwill."

Drawing his body into a coil, he shook his rattles and struck at Paisano with all his might! Quickly Paisano jumped back beyond his reach.

Again and again this happened—Paisano
moved in, teased his enemy to make him strike
again, but always jumped back just in time. Before long, Mr. Rattler became so tired that his
strike became weaker and weaker and slower
and slower.

Then Paisano began striking back, and striking hard! Again and again with his sharp bill he
pecked at Mr. Rattler's mouth and head, until at
last the snake began to back away, looking for a
hole into which he could crawl. But there was
none! And he was too tired to fight anymore.
This was the moment Paisano had been working toward! He grabbed the snake by the neck
and lifted him into the air, and beat his head
again and again upon a rock, until even in his
tail not one wiggle was left!

Just at that point, who do you suppose
marched out from a nearby bush? None other

21

than Mrs. Whippoorwill and her two little chicks, now safe and happy because of what the brave chaparral had done!

"We don't have any reward to give you," said Mr. Whippoorwill, "but you deserve a medal of honor. You are the bravest bird I have ever seen! And I do thank you for saving my chicks!"

"That's what I came to North America to do," said Paisano modestly. "I'm a pioneer, you know!"

"We'll never, never stop singing your praises," added Mrs. Whippoorwill as she led her little chicks back into the bush.

And the whippoorwills have kept that promise. Have you ever heard their song floating through the air at night?

"Whippoorwill, Whippoorwill,
Whippoorwill, Whippoorwill."

That is what it sounds like to us. But that is because we humans do not understand bird language. What every roadrunner hears (as does every other bird) is,

"Chaparral! Chaparral!
All is well! All is well!"

✳ ✳ ✳ ✳ ✳

# Prayer

*Dear God,*

*We do thank You for our country, and for the brave men and women who worked so hard and gave so much to make the United States of America the wonderful country that it is.*

*May we be brave and noble too, always standing for what is right and against what is wrong. Help us to grow up to be the kind of men and women you want us to be, and of whom our country will be proud. Amen.*

## What Does the Bible Say ...
# About Our World?

Deuteronomy 8:1-20; 11:8-19
Psalms 33:12
Matthew 28:18-20
John 4:37, 38
Acts 1:8; 22:24-29
Romans 13:1-7
Hebrews 11:32-40

## More to Think About
### The Children's Song

Land of our birth, our faith, our pride,
For whose dear sake our fathers died,
O Motherland, we pledge to thee
Our love and toil in the years to be.

Kipling

### So Long as There Are Homes

So long as there are homes to which men turn
At close of day;
So long as there are homes where children are,
Where women stay-
If love and loyalty and faith be found
Across those sills-
A stricken nation can recover from
Its gravest ills.
So long as there are homes where fires burn
And there is bread;
So long as there are homes where lamps are lit
And prayers are said;
Although people falter through the dark-
And nations grope-
With God himself back of these little homes-
We have sure hope.

—Grace Noll Crowell

# The Parable of
# The
# Flyaway Flamingo

*Suppose you were asked to do something that you knew you should not do—would you have the courage to say "no"? And if those who asked you kept on urging you, and if someone finally called you "chicken," then would you give in?*

*While you are thinking about these questions, let me tell you a story.*

\* \* \* \* \*

Freddie Flamingo was really a lucky bird, growing up in Highland Park where he had police protection day and night! But there was a time when Freddie didn't think this was so wonderful.

How proud Mr. and Mrs. Flamingo were of their little rooster! From the day he hopped out of his shell, they watched over him with tender love, and by the time he was a month old they were giving him swimming lessons in the beautiful blue lake in the park.

One of their best friends was Mr. Bull Frog. The first time he saw Freddie, he said in his deep voice, "Wonderful son, wonderful son!"

The flamingoes were gorgeous birds, and so graceful in the water that people came from far and near just to see them swimming together.

"Look at the cute little one," they said. "He can swim almost as well as the two big ones."

Before long, Mr. and Mrs. Flamingo were

25

teaching Freddie to fly—but only for short trips around the lake.

"It isn't safe to fly outside the park," they said to him. "That is why the park superintendent clipped your wings. You see, there are very few flamingoes left in the world. There are hunters outside the park who kill us to get our gorgeous pink feathers for women's hats. Besides," they added, "where could we be happier than in this lovely park?"

Deep down in his heart, Freddie knew they were right, but as he grew older he heard the crows in the trees outside cawing about the horrible northern weather, the jays screaming about "Bird Rights" and "Freedom Flights," and the ducks quacking about their plans to fly south for the winter, and Freddie began to think that maybe they were right and his parents were wrong. He wanted to see the world and experience all the things that the other birds had experienced.

One afternoon, Clarence McDuck waddled up to Freddie. "How about flying to Florida with us?" he asked. "We're starting tomorrow at sun-up from the other side of the lake."

"But my parents have told me it isn't safe to fly outside the park," Freddie answered.

"Aw, boop-boop-boop-bottom-chew!" Clarence quacked. "What do they know about the world when they've never been outside the park themselves? Besides, don't you have any mind of your own? What are you, anyway, a chicken?"

That was the word that did it! "I am *not* a chicken!" exploded Freddie. "My wings are wider than yours and I can outfly you ducks any day! I'll be on the other side of the lake in the morning and show you!"

All night long, Mr. Frog, who had heard every word of this "bird-versation," called in his deep voice, "Don't do it, don't do it, don't do it!" But Freddie's mind was made up. The next morning before Mr. and Mrs. Flamingo were awake, Freddie slipped off his roost, swam quietly across the lake, and a few minutes later, spread his wings and took off with the ducks, heading south.

Only Mr. Owl, who was coming home from an all-night blinking party, saw him leave.

"Hoot, hoot!" he called. "What's up?"

"We're off to Florida," Freddie shouted back. "Yippie!"

With that, Mr. Owl just crawled into his nest in a hollow tree, blinked his eyes three more times, and fell asleep.

Before long, Freddie found that no matter how hard he tried, he couldn't keep up with the ducks. He had forgotten about his clipped wings. The faster he flapped them, the more weary he became.

"Wait for me!" he called.

"Thought you could outfly a duck any day!" Clarence quacked. "We'll wait for you in Florida! Quack, quack!" (Which is a duck's way of saying, "Ha, ha!").

Now Freddie was alone, flying slower and slower and sinking lower and lower toward the ground. In front of him he saw a large building, which happened to be a bus station. Outside were several buses, and on the side of each was a picture of a large dog. Beside the dog, written in big bright letters was,

"Just take a bus
And leave the driving to us."

"Great luck!" Freddie said to himself as he landed on top of a bus labeled, "Florida Express." "I'll *ride* to Florida!"

The bus driver was the first to see him. "A pink flamingo!" he exclaimed as he grabbed for Freddie's legs. "How my wife would love those feathers for a hat!"

Freddie jumped back just in time. Soon he was running and flying through the bus station with more and more people trying to catch him.

Then he heard someone shout, "Here come

28

the police; let them handle it!" Sure enough, there were two men in blue coats coming toward him, each with a pistol hanging from his belt and a stick in his hand.

Freddie was really frightened now! More than once he had heard the crows and the jays chattering and warning each other about humans, so now he was sure he was going to be caught.

In a corner at the back of the bus station, he saw a little room and rushed in to hide. It was a telephone booth and on the wall just above him was a phone. "If I could only call my parents," he fretted, as he tried to dial Lakeside 38924.

But before he could finish, the two policemen were at the door. To his surprise, their voices were kind. "Take it easy, "Pinky," one of them said quietly. "We won't hurt you. You should know that this bus station is no place for a pink flamingo!"

Then the officers gently picked Freddie up, put him in a big cardboard box and carried him to their waiting patrol car.

Freddie was still frightened. "They're taking me to jail," he said to himself. "I'll be charged with disturbing the peace, booked as a delinquent flyaway, and claw-printed like a common criminal! Why didn't I listen to Mr. Bull Frog instead of to Clarence McDuck?"

But, as you may have guessed, it was not to jail that the policemen took Freddie, but right back to Highland Park.

"Here's your pink flamingo," they said to the park superintendent. "We heard over our radio that he was lost. Cornered him in the bus station downtown. Have no idea how he got there! Shall we put him back in the lake?"

"Not yet," said the superintendent. "First we must make sure that he never tries that flyaway stunt again."

Then, reaching into his desk drawer, he pulled out a pair of shears.

"But over the radio we heard that his wings were already clipped," said the policeman.

"Yes, but apparently not close enough," the superintendent replied. Then he said to Freddie, "Okay, smart bird! This won't hurt anything except your pride, but it should teach you a lesson." Then, whack! Off came six inches from Freddie's left wing! "Now we'll see how far you can fly with one wing six inches shorter than the other!"

Freddie knew he deserved that whack, so he really didn't mind it. He knew that from now on, no matter what the jays, crows, and ducks said, he would never again try to fly away!

When the park superintendent turned him loose a few minutes later, he made straight for the lake.

His mother and father had been looking for him everywhere all morning and were so glad to see him that they didn't scold him or ask any questions. They just wrapped their long necks around him and wept for joy!

Then Mr. Flamingo said, "Freddie, you must be really hungry."

Then down under the water went his head, and up he came with a nice minnow which he beaked over to Freddie.

On the bank close by, under a big lily leaf, Mr. Bull Frog was sitting, but not sleeping. He usually did not open his mouth to say anything except at night, but today he was overjoyed at what he saw and heard. He grinned from ear to ear, and opening wide his big mouth he sang in his deep bass voice, "Welcome home! Welcome home! Welcome home!"

✳ ✳ ✳ ✳ ✳

# Prayer

*Dear God,*

*We pray for wisdom to know the difference between right and wrong. And when we do know, make us strong enough to stand for the right, no matter what others may do. And give us the courage to do the right thing no matter what others may say. And please help us to say "No", when it needs to be said. Like Daniel, may we dare to stand alone, dare to have a purpose firm, dare to make it known. Amen.*

31

# About Obedience?

Exodus 20:12
Psalms 119:9
Proverbs 1:10, 15; 3:1-4
Ecclesiastes 12:1, 13
Daniel 1:8-21
Matthew 6:13
Luke 4:1-13
Luke 15:11-24
Ephesians 6:1-3, 10-18
James 1:14, 15; 4:7

# More to Think About

## House and Home

A house is built of logs and stone,
Of piles and posts and piers;
A home is built of loving deeds
That stand a thousand years.
—Hugo

## Home, Sweet Home

'Mid pleasures and palaces though we may
  roam,
Be it ever so humble, there's no place like home.
A charm from the sky seems to hallow us there,
Which, seek through the world, is ne'er met
  with elsewhere.
Home, home, sweet, sweet home!
There's no place like Home!
—Payne

32

# God Bless Our Home

Eternal Father, who has given
To homes on earth foretaste of Heaven,
Whose gentle Spirit from above
Doth breathe Thy peace in hearts that love;
While here we bide, or far we roam,
Hear this our prayer: God bless our home!

Eternal Father, ever near,
With arm outstretched and listening ear,
Whose mercy keeps, whose power defends
Our sons, our daughters, and our friends,
While here we bide, or far we roam,
Hear this our prayer: God bless our home!

Robert Freeman


## From, **Prayer for the Home**

Lord, this humble house we'd keep
Sweet with play and calm with sleep.
Help us so that we may give
Beauty to the lives we live.
Let Thy love and let Thy grace
Shine upon our dwelling place.

Edgar A. Guest

# The Parable of

# The Boastful Turtle

*Do you know boys and girls who talk too much about themselves? Children who seem to be always boasting about what they have done or what they can do? And does their boasting make you like them more, or just the opposite?*

*Do you sometimes talk too much about yourself? And does your boasting sometimes get you into trouble? That's exactly what happened to Snapper, a young sea turtle.*

*Let me tell you about him.*

\* \* \* \* \*

Snapper spent most of his time in the ocean. But now and then he would crawl out onto the beach where he had been hatched, to visit with the birds.

As he listened to them chattering about how high they could fly, and how beautiful the ocean and the fields were when seen from away up in the sky, he found himself wishing that he too could fly and see with his own eyes the wonderful sights they kept chirping about.

But of course he had no wings. Then one night there flashed into his mind a clever idea. The next morning he found a round stick about three feet long, carried it over to Mr. & Mrs. Gull,

and pleaded, "Please, Mr. and Mrs. Gull, won't you take me for a ride up in the sky?"

Then he went on to explain what he had in mind. "You could take hold of one end of this stick with your claws. Mr. Gull, and you, Mrs. Gull, could do the same with the other end. My jaws are strong and I could hold on to the middle with my teeth while you flapped your wings and lifted me up and over the waves toward the sky."

"Why, Snapper, what a wild idea!" exclaimed Mr. Gull.

"It's new, but not wild," said Snapper. "We could call your service, 'The Wington Airlift!' I'm sure you would find other customers later. Think of the crabs, the clams, the oysters, the frogs, and all the other creatures that don't have wings, but who also wish they could fly!"

Now when it came to business matters, Mr. Gull was no bird's fool. To own and operate "The Wington Airlift," he said to himself, would indeed be much more exciting than his present business, which was operating "The Gullible Fish Market." It could be more profitable too.

So he said to Snapper, "What will you pay us for a fifteen-minute ride?"

Snapper, of course, had no money and no fish, clams, oysters, or shrimp to offer for his ride. So for a minute he didn't know what to answer. Then an idea came into his mind and he said, "I could baby-sit beside your nest and guard your chicks while you take up passengers." And that was the agreement they made!

That very afternoon a strange sight appeared in the sky above Wington Beach. The birds on the shore looked up in amazement. "It's a flying saucer from another world," some said. Others took off on their wings to get a better look. Mr. Duck and Mr. Loon flew in quite close and could hardly believe what they saw. Mr. and Mrs. Gull were sailing through the air with Snapper between them, holding the stick tight in his jaws! And that was not all; trailing behind him, fastened to his tail, was a bright streamer that read, "Wington Airlift!"

"What a brilliant idea!" exclaimed Mr. Duck.

"I wonder who was smart enough to think of it?" said Mr. Loon.

Snapper's little chest, swelling with pride, pushed hard against his shell. His eyes sparkled like two little stars. Opening his mouth, he shouted, "I did!"

Then, ooops! He was plunging down, down toward the ocean, the bright streamer, like a

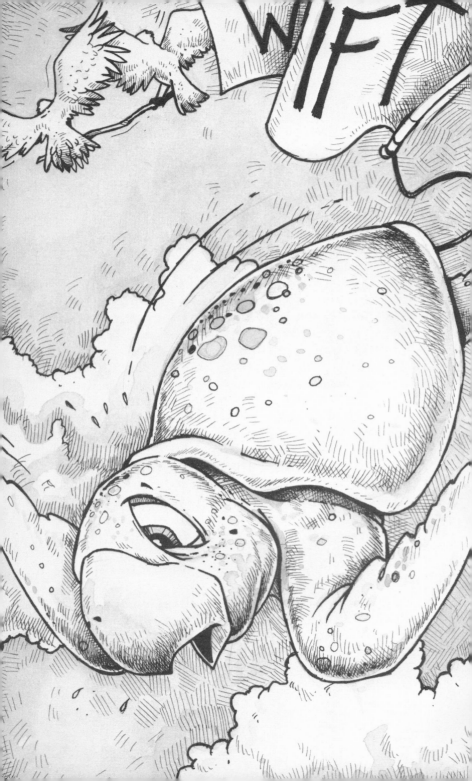

punctured balloon, sailing behind him. In a flash "The Wington Airlift" had become "The Wington Airdrop!"

Being a sea turtle, Snapper was not hurt by his plunge into the ocean. Only was pride was bruised! But just before he hit the water, Polly Porpoise, who was fishing close by and had just come up for a breath of air, heard him say, "If only I had kept my big mouth shut!"

When Pastor Penguin heard the story, his face lit up with a smile. "A perfect illustration for my next sermon," he said to himself.

And so it was, for the text on which he was working was Proverbs chapter 16, verse 18, where it is said, "Pride goes before destruction, and a haughty spirit before a fall."

\* \* \* \* \*

## Prayer

*Dear God,*

*Help us never to forget that all our opportunities, talents, and abilities are gifts that we have received from You, and they are, therefore, things that should make us thankful, but not boastful.*

*May we be quick to praise others, but slow to praise ourselves. And when others praise us, may we be grateful, but not proud. Amen.*

## What Does the Bible Say ...
# About Boasting?

Proverbs 11:2; 15:33; 16:18; 29:23
Matthew 18:3, 4
Luke 14:7-11; 18:9-14
John 13:3-17
Romans 12:3
Philippians 2:3-11
1 Peter 5:5

## More to Think About

### The Shepherd Boy's Song

He that is down need fear no fall,
He that is low on pride;
He that is humble ever shall
Have God to be his guide.

Bunyan

## Humility

Though heaven is high, the gate is low,
And he who comes in there must bow;
Lofty looks shall ne'er
Find entrance there.

Washbourne

## The Happiest Heart

The happiest heart that ever beat
    Was in some quiet breast
That found the common daylight sweet
    And left to Heaven the rest.

John Vance Cheney

# The Parable of
# The Runaway Raindrops

*Do you like sports? Almost all of us do! But we don't like rules, do we? We have minds and wills of our own and don't want to be told what to do and what not to do!*

*Yet, what would sports be without rules? Try to imagine a tennis match, for example, without lines on the court, or a net! Or a baseball game with no bases and no umpire! Or football without lines and goalposts or a referee!*

*And what would happen to an athlete who refused to play according to the rules of the game? Or, what happens to one who is careless about the rules of health—such as regular sleep and exercise, nourishing food, and no smoking, alcohol, or drugs?*

*Has God given us any rules by which to live? What happens if we obey them? What happens if we ignore them?*

*Perhaps the story that follows will help you to answer these questions.*

*"Little drops of water, little grains of sand*
*Make the mighty ocean, and the pleasant land."*

*But not all drops of water reach the mighty ocean! This is the story of some who did, and of some who did not, and why.*

\* \* \* \* \*

41

Away above the mountains one night, a storm cloud was getting ready to send her raindrops down to the earth. The lightning and thunder had been ready for some time, but before the raindrops began to fall, their mother, the cloud, gathered them around her and said, "My children, you are ready for a great adventure. You are going on a long journey to visit your father, the ocean. Down on the earth, you will run into many dangers, and if you are not careful, you may get lost and never meet your father.

"Soon after you reach the earth, you will find yourselves flowing in the bed of a little stream. In time the little stream will become a creek, and later a river. Sometimes it will flow slowly, sometimes very fast, sometimes straight, and sometimes in great curves, but always it will be carrying you toward the ocean!

"On each side of the stream there will be a bank to keep you from breaking out and getting lost, and to steer you on your way. Remember, dear children, make it a rule to stay as near the center of the stream as you can, and never, never leap over a bank!"

Then she kissed them tenderly and handed them over to a soft, cool breeze. And the wind, like a great airplane, carried them away, then down, down, down—until they landed, ever so gently in the forest on a high mountainside. A little later, as they were racing down the mountainside in a clear, cool stream, some of the raindrops said to one another, "What does our mother know about the earth? We don't like her advice about staying in the center of the stream! These banks on either side of us make the stream too narrow. They hem us in! Don't we have the right to do what we want to? Aren't we free? Let's break out and see the world before

42

going on to find our father. Let's do our own thing first!"

They grumbled and complained until some of the more unhappy ones finally lunged at a soft, low place in the bank, and broke through.

As they poured down the hillside in a path of their own choosing, they danced and laughed. "Isn't this fun?" they asked one another. "Now we are truly free! This is really living! Going where we like and doing what we please! No rules, only just being free!"

And they mocked the other raindrops who stayed in the bed of the stream. "You are crazy," they shouted. "Come on out and away and have fun with us! You don't know what you're missing. Our mother doesn't know everything!"

By and by they came to a low place in the valley and, being very tired by now, they spread themselves out and lay very still. Soon, the sun's hot tongue began to lick them up, and quite a few of the wayward raindrops simply disappeared. That night, wild animals came down for a drink and swallowed some of them. Later, an ugly green scum spread itself over those that were left, and they gave out a bad smell, and bred gnats, mosquitoes, and snakes. People stayed away from the place, because it had become a foul swamp!

Such was the end that came to the raindrops that ignored their mother's advice and broke through the banks of the river. Their "great adventure" turned out to be a "great disaster."

But the other raindrops, who remembered to stay within the banks of the river as their mother had told them, were running merrily on! They were on their way to the ocean!

Once, they came to a great dam of stone and concrete. It held them back for a little while, but

44

soon they found a door through a big pipe, called a flume. It smooth sides were narrower and stronger than the banks of the river, but into it they leaped, plunging straight down and making a mighty waterfall. At the foot of the waterfall, they jumped on the blades of a great wheel, and the wheel spun round and round, faster and faster, and turned a huge machine called a dynamo. The dynamo made electricity that brought light and heat into the factories and stores and homes of people for miles and miles!

Later they came to a flour mill. Laughing with glee, they ran toward the mill and leaped down on the mill's waterwheel. Thus they turned the wheel, and the wheel turned the mill, and the mill ground the grain, and the grain became flour, and men and women and little children had bread.

Still later, they flowed quietly through great fields of corn and wheat and beautiful meadows. Farmers sat down beside the bank to rest and eat their lunch and said to one another, "If it were not for the water in the river, we would not have our fertile fields and bountiful crops and the green grass for our cows and sheep and horses."

But best of all, the raindrops who had listened to their mother and stayed inside the banks of the stream, came at last to the mouth of the river, and there, waiting for them was their father, the ocean! As he stretched out his open arms to welcome them, they ran with quiet ripples of joy to meet him!

Then he lifted them up on his great, powerful arms, the waves, and carried them to a sandy white beach. There children and young people were waiting to welcome them. The children laughed in glee as they ran to dive into the water and ride the waves back to the shore!

As the waves rolled back from the beach, the raindrops made it a game to play with the fish, crabs, shrimp, and other sea creatures—all of whom were wonderful swimmers.

Then came the fun the raindrops enjoyed most of all—when lightning was seen in the sky and the roll of thunder was heard.

"It is the voice of your mother," said their father. "She is coming to visit us. We will go to meet her."

At such times, their father's arms became stronger than ever and he would lift them higher and higher upon mighty waves toward the cloud above them. It was like a jolly picnic with both ocean and cloud happy beyond words in their reunion with each other and their children!

46

Such was the reward experienced by the rain-drops that listened to the advice of their mother, and stayed within the banks of the stream all the way to the ocean. Their "great adventure" turned out to also be a "great achievement."

\* \* \* \* \*

## Prayer

*Dear God,*

*We thank You for rules because now we see that they are meant to do for us what banks do for a river; rules protect us and guide us on our way.*

*Help us to choose wisely the rules by which we intend to live, and then help us to obey them, not only carefully but cheerfully. Thus in due time, may we become who and what You want us to be, and find and fulfill Your highest purpose for our lives. Amen.*

**What Does the Bible Say ...**
## About What Is Expected of Us?

Deuteronomy 5:1-21, 32, 33
Joshua 1:7
Psalms 19:7-11; 119:1-6
Proverbs 3:1, 2
Ecclesiastes 12:1, 13
Matthew 7:13, 14; 16:24, 25
Philippians 3:13, 14
Hebrews 12:1, 2

# More to Think About

## Come Thou My Light

Come, Thou my Light, that I may see
   Thy truth divine, Thy love so free.
Dispel the clouds of doubt and sin
   And let the face of God shine in.

Come Thou my Life, that I may be
   Made one in living faith with Thee.
Renew my will and make it Thine,
   Thou living source of life divine.

Come Thou my Guide, that I may know
   The way my seeking soul should go:
And never from Thee let me stray,
   Thyself the Life, the Truth, the Way.

Come Thou my King, and I will make
   My heart a shrine, for Thy dear sake:
Until this earthly life of mine
   Shall be forever wholly Thine.
                    Hugh Thomson Kerr


## Follow Me!

Who answers Christ's insistent call
Must give himself, his life, his all,
Without one backward look.
Who sets his hand unto the plow,
And glances back with anxious brow,
His calling hath mistook.
Christ claims him wholly for His own;
He must be Christ's, and Christ's alone.
                    John Oxenham

# The Ways

To every man there openeth
A way, and ways, and a way.
And the high soul climbs the high Way,
And the low soul gropes the low,
And in between, on the misty flats,
The rest drift to and fro.
To every man there openeth
A high way, and a low.
And every man decideth
The way his soul shall go.

John Oxenham

# Christ's Bondservant

Make me a captive, Lord,
    And then I shall be free;
Force me to render up my sword,
    And I shall conqueror be.
I sink in life's alarms
    When by myself I stand;
Imprison me within Thine arms,
    And strong shall be my hand.

My will is not my own
    Till Thou hast made it Thine;
If it would reach a monarch's throne
    It must its crown resign!
It only stands unbent
    Amid the clashing strife,
When on Thy bosom it has leant
    And found in Thee its life.

George Matheson

# The Parable of
# The Spunky Squirrel

*If someone were to say that you have a lot of spunk, would you be pleased? Would you feel that a nice thing had been said about you, or just the opposite? What does the word "spunk" mean, anyway? Perhaps you will find the answer in this story about a little squirrel whose name was Spunky.*

\* \* \* \* \*

Timber Bear had a birthday coming up soon, and Spunky Squirrel kept asking himself, "What can I give for a present?"

Timber and Spunky were great friends and enjoyed many walks through the forest together. Timber was very much interested in birds and seemed to know almost everything there was to know about them. In their walks together, he taught Spunky how to identify the different kinds of birds by their songs and also by the colors of their feathers.

Over the years, Timber had made it his hobby to collect bird feathers. On this particular afternoon, when Timber and Spunky were almost home from their walk, Timber said, "Would you like to come into my den and see my feather collection?"

Spunky was delighted, and once inside he could hardly believe his eyes! Fastened to the wall all around Timber's den were more than a hundred feathers of all sizes and colors. Underneath each feather was the name of the bird to which it had belonged.

"Wow!" exclaimed Spunky. "I had no idea there were so many different kinds of birds in the world!"

"Oh, there are a great many more than these," said Timber. "Look at this."

As he spoke, he opened an Audubon bird book and showed Spunky the picture of a gorgeous peacock. "See Spunky, in his feathers are found all the colors of the rainbow. And the feathers are so large and beautiful they are not called feathers at all, but plumes! How I wish I could find one of *those* to add to my collection!"

As Spunky walked home later, he said to himself, "That's it! Timber is the best friend I have in all the world, and he has taught me almost everything I know about birds. I must find a peacock plume for his birthday present!"

Timber had taught Spunky another thing too,

> When a task is once begun,
> Never leave it 'til it's done;
> Be it great or be it small,
> Do it well, or not at all.

The next morning before the sun was up, Spunky jumped out of bed, washed his face, brushed his hair, cracked and ate five pecans for his breakfast (from the supply in his nest), and dashed away in search of a peacock plume.

First he climbed an oak tree and knocked on Mr. Tappy Woodpecker's door. "I have never even heard of a peacock," was Tappy's answer to Spunky's question, "and I know all the birds in the forest. Now there is a cock-a-doodle-doo that lives on a nearby farm. He wakes up all the other birds, and the animals too, by crowing early in the morning. But his feathers are small and quite plain. They would never be called plumes."

52

Next, Spunky knocked on the door of Mr. Owl, who was thought to be the wisest, as well as the laziest, bird in the forest.

"Great day in the morning!" exclaimed Mr. Owl, blinking his eyes in response to Spunky's question. "You must really want a peacock plume to come knocking on my door so early in the morning. I had just gone to bed—I work the night shift, you know. But come on in and close the door; the light hurts my eyes."

Once inside, Mr. Owl explained to Spunky that he was wasting his time looking for a peacock plume in the forest.

"The peacock," he said, "is a native of India. You will not find one in any field or forest here. But I did hear," he added, "that there is one in the zoo over in Kalamazoo. But of course, that is too far for you to go with your little feet and short legs. Too bad you don't have wings. Why, I suppose Kalamazoo is ten miles away, as the crow flies."

It was the expression, "as the crow flies" that gave Spunky his next ideas. As fast as his little legs could take him, he scurried up to Mr. Crow's nest—although he had to climb to the top of a tall pine tree to reach it.

Mr. Crow listened to Spunky's story, then said, "As a matter of fact, I have a business trip this very morning that will take me close to Kalamazoo. I'm flying over there to inspect a new cornfield I have heard about. So if you would like to come along, I'll fly you over, and drop you off at the zoo."

Now Spunky had never been on a birdplane before, and he shook all over at the thought of sailing through the air on Mr. Crow's back. But so eager was he to find a peacock plume for his friend, Timber, that he thanked Mr. Crow and

climbed aboard. Soon they were high in the sky on their way to Kalamazoo.

Although Spunky trembled with fright all the way, he clung tightly to Mr. Crow's feathers, and soon they arrived safely at the zoo.

Mr. Peacock was quite flattered when Spunky told him about seeing his picture in Timber's Audubon bird book. He spread his plumes in the sunlight in the shape of a great fan so Spunky could see and admire their gorgeous colors.

But when Spunky asked if he might have one to take to his friend Timber, Mr. Peacock folded up his fan and said, "Suppose we make a deal. You like my plumes, and as a matter of fact, I am very fond of pecans—quite a treat for a bird who has to put up day after day with stewed zoo food! What do you say to this; you may have your choice of any plume in my fan, if you will bring me a pound of your pecans. I have heard that you squirrels have plenty of nuts."

Spunky was glad to close the deal. He remembered he had over ten pounds of pecans stored up back home in preparation for winter and said to himself, "I'll hardly miss only one pound!"

He was so happy he could hardly wait to tell Mr. Crow about his good fortune. But as he took his place on Mr. Crow's back for the return trip, Mr. Peacock came over and said, "Of course, the pecans must be shelled—I have no teeth for cracking nuts, you know!"

On their way home, Spunky said to Mr. Crow, "A pound of shelled pecans—that means a lot of work! And it may take all the pecans I have. But, I don't mind," he added with a smile. "Think of it, Mr. Crow, I will get my choice of all those gorgeous plumes in Mr. Peacock's fan!"

Spunky was right about the hard work involved in cracking and shelling an entire pound of pecans. As soon as he got home, he started to work, but it was midnight before he finished. He was right about another thing, too. It took all his pecans to make the full pound of shelled ones!

He was very tired as he poured the shelled nuts into a bag and tied it with a string. Then crawled into bed, hugging the bag close to his side to guard it all night!

Early the next morning, Spunky hopped aboard Mr. Crow and was soon back in the zoo.

Mr. Peacock was quite pleased with the bag of pecans and promptly spread out his plumes so Spunky could make his selection. His choice was a large one in the center of the fan, which he touched with his little paw. Mr. Peacock then twisted his long neck backward, took hold of the plume with his bill, gave it a quick jerk, and handed it over to Spunky.

A few minutes later, clutching the precious plume in his mouth, Spunky was once again on Mr. Crow's back, high in the sky on their way home.

As they landed on the top of the pine tree beside Mr. Crow's nest, Spunky said, "Mr. Crow, I don't know how to thank you. You've made me very happy. I wish I could pay you, but I don't have any pecans left."

"You don't owe me a thing," said Mr. Crow, "except to keep on being a spunky little squirrel. As for the pecans, we crows don't go for nuts, you know. Our favorite food is corn on the cob!"

Spunky climbed down the tree head first, clinging to his precious plume, and hurried home. Just after sunrise the next morning, he knocked on the door of Timber's den.

As Timber opened the door, Spunky exclaimed, "Happy Birthday!" and handed him the peacock plume. And now it was Timber who couldn't believe his eyes. "Why Spunky! What a gorgeous plume! Where in the world did you get it?"

"From Mr. Peacock in the Kalamazoo Zoo," Spunky answered, and then told Timber the entire story.

When he finished, Timber lifted him up, set him on his knee and said, "Spunky, I'm so proud to have this plume that I am going to frame it and hang it in the very center of my collection. But I am even more proud of you and of all you did to get it. You have proved that 'where there's a will, there's a way.'"

Then he added, "You have proved another thing too—that the name 'Spunky' is just right for you. You are really a spunky little squirrel and a wonderful friend!"

# Prayer

*Dear God,*

*Please keep us from ever being lazy. When there is something we should do, no matter how hard it may be, may we get busy about doing it, instead of looking for an excuse to keep from doing it.*

*Also, keep us from putting off until later something we should do now, or from not finishing a task we have started. Help us always, To do our best, And give our best, And meet every test With courage and zest. Amen.*

## What Does the Bible Say ...
## About Gifts and Perseverance?

Matthew 7:7, 8; 13:44-46
Luke 18:1-8
Romans 12:10-13
1 Corinthians 9:24-27
Philippians 3:12-14
Colossians 3:23, 24
2 Timothy 2:3-7, 15; 4:7, 8
Hebrews 12:1, 2

# More to Think About

### It Couldn't Be Done

Somebody said that it couldn't be done,
But he with a chuckle replied
That maybe it couldn't, but he would be one
Who wouldn't say so till he'd tried.
So he buckled right in with the trace of a grin ...
He started to sing as he tackled the thing
That couldn't be done, and he did it!

Guest

# The Psalm Of Life

The heights by great men reached and kept
Were not attained by sudden flight;
But they, while their companions slept,
Were toiling upward in the night.
Let us then be up and doing,
With a heart for any fate;
Still achieving, still pursuing,
Learn to labor and to wait.

Longfellow

# Fight The Good Fight

Fight the good fight with all thy might,
Christ is thy strength, and Christ thy right;
Lay hold on life, and it shall be
Thy joy and crown eternally.

Run the straight race through God's good grace,
Lift up thine eyes and seek His face;
Life with its way before us lies,
Christ is the path, and Christ the prize.

Cast care aside, lean on thy Guide,
His boundless mercy will provide;
Trust, and thy trusting soul shall prove
Christ is its life, and Christ its love.

Faint not nor fear, His arms are near,
He changeth not and thou art dear;
Only believe, and thou shalt see
That Christ is all in all to thee.

John S. B. Monsell

# The Parable of
# The Selfish Birds

*If you were in a country where there are a lot of monkeys, and you wanted to catch one, what kind of trap would you use?*

*I have heard that all you need to catch a monkey is a milk bottle, fastened by a strong rope to a tree, with two or three nuts inside the bottle.*

*Before long, one of the monkeys would come by. Seeing the nuts and wanting them, he would push his hand into the mouth of the bottle and close his fist around the nuts! To get free, all he would have to do would be to turn the nuts loose and slip his hand back out again. But no! He wouldn't do that! So determined would he be to keep the nuts and not let any other monkey have them, that he'd hold them tight in his fist! And as long as he held to the nuts, he would be caught in the trap!*

*Now, let me ask you a question—and think twice before you answer—what is it that really traps the monkey? Is it the nuts, or his own selfishness and greed?*

*This question brings us to a story about the birds of Wington and how they found that there is a much better way to live than to be selfish and greedy!*

\* \* \* \* \*

Bushy Squirrel liked his name, because he was proud of his wide, fluffy tail. But none of the birds called him "Bushy." They called him such names as "Pesky," "Thief," or "Robber," because they didn't like him at all!

Every morning, Bushy would come to the bird feeder in Mrs. Kindheart's yard. Then, no matter how much the birds screamed, he would climb up the pole and have his breakfast, while they had to wait until he left.

One day, Mr. Woodpecker drilled holes along the edge of the feeder with his sharp bill, spelling out the words, "FOR THE BIRDS ONLY!" But that didn't faze Bushy! The next morning he just put his claws into the holes to keep from falling and stayed twice as long!

The birds chattered angrily about the problem until Mr. Cardinal finally came up with the idea that worked. Flying over to the Atlantic Fish Oil Company one afternoon, he said to Mr. Gull, "I want to buy a quart of your slickest oil."

"Here you are," said Mr. Gull, handing him a can marked "Triple—A Slick." "This oil is guaranteed to stay slick in rain, snow, or sunshine."

Five minutes later, using a turkey feather for a brush, Mr. Cardinal was painting the pole of the birdfeeder with the Triple—A Slick oil. By the time he was finished, almost every bird in Wington was watching, all of them chirping and chattering, all aflutter over Mr. Cardinal's clever idea!

Early the next morning they were back, hiding in the trees, waiting to see what would happen when Bushy arrived.

They did not have to wait long, for just after sunup they saw him coming, hopping merrily along, straight toward their feeder. When he was just three feet away, he looked up and saw that the feeder had been freshly filled the night before by Mrs. Kindheart. Bushy twitched his tail three times in joyful expectation, and then, wearing a broad smile, he leaped high into the air and onto the pole. But this time his sharp claws did not hold. Straight downward he slid, landing with a thump on the ground below!

At this point, the birds let go—they chirped, they cackled, they squawked, they mocked!

"Try again, try again," they cried.

And Bushy did! Their mocking laughter made him only more determined. He tried from a point closer to the pole, leaped higher toward the top—and slid down the slippery pole faster and hit the ground harder than before!

Again and again the same thing happened, Bushy leaped and slid and the birds laughed and mocked.

At last he gave up and climbed to a nearby limb to rest, twitch his tail, and study what his next move should be.

Suddenly, Mrs. Woodpecker gave a shrill scream! Immediately all eyes were turned toward her, and then toward the cause of her scream; Slinky Snake! He was crawling along a limb straight toward Mrs. Woodpecker's nest in the hole of a tree, not far from the birdfeeder.

By this time, Mrs. Woodpecker was in birdsterics. "Stop him, stop him," she cried. "Don't let him get my baby chicks!" Several brave birds tried to stop him by screaming and diving close to Slinky's head. But Slinky was determined. Inch by inch he slithered closer and closer to the Woodpecker nest.

Soon he was close enough to see inside. Licking out his tongue and looking hungrily at the nearest of three little woodpeckers, he pushed in his head.

62

Then suddenly he was hit by something from above, so hard that it felt like a ton of bricks! He lost his balance and fell straight to the ground! Not until he landed did Slinky see what had hit him.

While all eyes had been on Slinky, Bushy had slipped through the trees, climbing and jumping from limb to limb, and had posted himself (just in time) on a limb ten feet above Mrs. Woodpecker's nest.

When Slinky's head went in, Bushy came down, dive-bombing him with all his might! His sharp claws were still holding Slinky by the neck when they hit the ground, and before he let loose, Bushy made Slinky promise to eat only flies, gnats, bugs, and mosquitoes for the rest of his life and never, never to climb a tree or go near a bird's nest again! Then, but not 'till then, did he let go!

The birds listened carefully, and watched as Slinky disappeared into a nearby thicket. Then they began to feel ashamed of how they had treated Bushy.

Flying down beside him, Mrs. Woodpecker put a wing over Bushy's shoulder and said, "How brave you are! How can I ever repay you for saving my little chicks?"

Then Mr. Cardinal, speaking for all the birds, invited Bushy to come and have breakfast with them. "You can't climb up, but our food can come down," he said. And the other birds, chirping and singing gratefully to Bushy, pushed choice seeds over the edge of their feeder down to the foot of the pole. Bushy ate until he couldn't swallow one bite more. Then, before he hopped away, the birds invited him to come back and have breakfast with them every morning.

64

"And you won't have to eat on the ground anymore," Mrs. Woodpecker promised. That very afternoon, she and Mr. Woodpecker did a very wonderful thing. With their sharp bills they drilled holes in the slick pole so Bushy could use them as steps and climb up to the feeder whenever he wished. Best of all, they also drilled another word in front of the sign they had made earlier. This word completely changed the meaning because the sign now reads, *"NOT* FOR THE BIRDS ONLY!"

✳ ✳ ✳ ✳ ✳

# Prayer

*Dear God,*
*We know the world and everything in it be-*
*longs to You, so all the good things we have*
*and enjoy are Your gifts to us. Help us to re-*
*member that they are not only ours to keep,*
*but also to share.*
*Do teach us to be kind and generous to every-*
*one, especially to those who have less than we*
*do. Every day may we remember, until we*
*learn how to give, we don't know how to live.*
*Amen*

## What Does the Bible Say ...
# About Selfishness and Sharing?

Proverbs 19:17; 22:9
Matthew 25:34-40
Luke 6:30-36; 10:25-37; 12:13-21
John 6:5-13
Acts 4:32-35; 20:35
2 Corinthians 9:6, 7
1 Timothy 6:17-19

# More to Think About

## If I Can Stop One Heart From Breaking

If today I can stop one heart from breaking,
I shall not have lived in vain;
If today I can ease one life from aching,
Or cool one person's pain,
Or help one fainting robin
Into his nest again,
I shall not have lived in vain.

Dickinson (adapted)

66

# A Morning Prayer

Let me today do something that will take
   A little sadness from the world's vast store
And may I be so favored as to make
   Of joy's too scanty sum a little more.

Let me tonight look back across the span
   'Twixt dawn and dark, and to my conscience
     say—
Because of some good act to beast or man—
   "The world is better that I lived today."
                  Ella Wheeler Wilcox

# I Shall Not Pass Again This Way

The bread that bringeth strength I want to give,
The water pure that bids the thirsty live;
I want to help the fainting day by day;
I'm sure I shall not pass again this way.

I want to give to others hope and faith;
I want to do all that the Master saith;
I want to live aright from day to day;
I'm sure I shall not pass again this way.
                  Ellen H. Underwood

# The Parable of
# The Merciful Retriever

*Do you know what a missionary is? Have you ever talked with one or heard one speak in your church? Do you know where missionaries go and what they do? Was Jesus a missionary? What would you think of having a special day to honor the missionaries from your church and to thank them for the wonderful things they do for others? Think about this idea as you hear the story of the grateful birds of marshland.*

\* \* \* \* \*

Well, would you believe it? The birds of Marshland once set aside a special day to honor, of all things, a dog! That's hard to believe, of course, because most birds are afraid of dogs and think of them as their enemies. But Russ Retriever was anything but an enemy of the birds. Amazingly, he had come to Marshland as a medical missionary!

Of course, the birds did not know this at first, so when he arrived in Marshland, Mrs. Mallard Duck called her ducklings to her side and said, "Quack, quack! He's a quack, I tell you! Keep away from him. Don't be fooled by that doctor's bag he carries and the white coat he wears! No bird is ever safe when a dog is around. Dogs are our enemies—all of them!"

The other birds squawked loud and long when Dr. Retriever went into the forest to get lumber. They were all afraid of him, but they were wrong about Russ Retriever. He was a friend of the birds, a doctor dog who had come to Marshland to build and manage his own hospital.

Dr. Retriever worked day after day, patiently and quietly building his hospital. Not once did he growl or bark back at the birds, although they screamed at him all day long.

Finally, his construction was finished, and there beside the lake stood the Audubon Mercy Hospital! Over the front door waved a Red Cross flag—a sign that medical help was available for any and all sick or wounded birds.

A few days after the hospital opened, the dreaded hunting season began. Hungers arrived in Marshland with their guns, and the birds scattered in all directions. Then it was that Dr. Retriever's merciful work began. From dawn till dark, he dashed here and there in search of wounded birds. Sometimes he would swim far out into the lake to rescue one. Gently he would take the wounded bird into his mouth and swim back to shore, then rush the bird to his hospital and there nurse it back to health.

Then an odd thing began to take place. Instead of flying away once their wounds were healed, quite a few birds asked Dr. Retriever if

they might stay and work as nurses or attendants. Others gratefully offered to build new rooms for sick and wounded birds. Before long, the Audubon Mercy Hospital was the largest and most important building in all of Marshland.

Then one day, Mr. Pheasant, the mayor of Marshland, and Mr. Mallard Duck, secretary of the council, put their heads together and hatched a wonderful idea.

"You know," began Mr. Pheasant, "I owe my life to Dr. Retriever. Both of my wings were broken when he rescued me from the lake."

"I owe him just as much as you do," said Mr. Duck. "Two years ago he removed a shot from my chest which had almost reached my heart. I still have the scar," he added, beaking his feathers aside to show it.

The next day Mr. Duck and Mr. Pheasant presented to the Marshland Council the idea they had hatched, which was to set aside a special day to honor Dr. Retriever for his great service to the birdmunity.

As a suitable gift Mr. Woodpecker, who was the leading architect in Marshland, and who had built himself a most unusual home in Oak Acres, came up with a winning suggestion. He reminded the council that Dr. Retriever had never taken time to build himself a home, but was living in the basement of his hospital.

"I make a motion," said Mr. Woodpecker, "that the birds of Marshland build him a home. I will gladly draw up the plans and supervise the project."

Every bird on the council fluttered a wing in favor of the motion, and the very next day Mr. Woodpecker, after searching through the forest, found a big tree near the hospital with a large hollow space near the bottom. "This is just what we need," he said.

Turning to the birds waiting to help, he explained what materials would be needed, and assigned various tasks to different birds. And away they flew into the forest, singing happily as they worked together!

Mrs. Quail and Mrs. Whippoorwill were put in charge of building Dr. Retriever's bed inside the hollow tree. This, they agreed, should simply be a nest large enough for Dr. Retriever to lie down in it and be comfortable.

"It must be strong," said Mrs. Whippoorwill as she wrapped ivy vines around the large sticks in the bottom to make it firm. "But also soft and comfortable," said Mrs. Quail, as she lined the bottom with grass, then added bits of string, cotton, and soft feathers.

To keep Dr. Retriever warm in winter, Mr. Crane found a red wool blanket left in a deserted lodge. He and Mr. Heron, flying side by side and holding it by their claws, brought it all the way to Dr. Retriever's new house.

Dr. Retriever was to have a bed outside too—a swinging hammock fastened by ropes to two small trees in front of his house. This hammock was made by Mrs. Goose and Mrs. Swan from a quilt brought from the same deserted lodge in which Mr. Crane had found the red blanket.

On the day after all the work was finished, the big event was a luncheon at the Ritsy Birdsy Plaza Hotel, to honor Dr. Retriever. Of course, all the birds had a seafood plate, but Dr. Retriever was served a sirloin steak two inches thick!

The main speech was made by Mayor Pheasant. He praised Dr. Retriever so much that the guest of honor found it hard to keep from wagging his tail under his chair! No bird could ever forget his final tribute, "Russ, you are the greatest because you gave the mostest!"

There was fun and laughter at the luncheon too. For example, Mr. Duck sang a funny little song, that began, "He's no quack in our almanac...." Then came the big surprise! Dr. Retriever was invited to climb aboard the "magic carpet," which was nothing but the red blanket that Mr. Crane and Mr. Heron had found in the hunter's lodge. Dr. Retriever was asked to lie down on it, which he did. Then four whooping cranes came up. "Ready," said Mayor Pheasant, as if they were starting a race, "one, two, three; fly!"

And the four cranes, each holding a corner of

the blanket in his claws, began to flap their wings! They lifted Dr. Retriever high into the air, and away they flew, like a four-motored airplane, followed by the birds of Marshland, all as happy as larks, heading straight for Dr. Retriever's house!

A few minutes later, in a landing as smooth as any bird could ever hope to see, the cranes set Dr. Retriever down in front of his new home. There, just over the door, he read with eyes that were by this time moist with tears, the tribute Mr. Woodpecker and Mr. Yellowhammer had neatly carved with their sharp bills,

> You set our bones
> And cured our fever;
> So here's your home,
> Dear Doctor Retriever.

＊ ＊ ＊ ＊ ＊

# Prayer

> *Dear God,*
> *If I can do some good today,*
> *If I can serve along life's way,*
> *If I can something helpful say,*
> *Dear God, may I do it!*
>
> *If I can right some human wrong,*
> *If I can make someone strong,*
> *If I can cheer with smile or song,*
> *Dear God, may I do it!*
>
> *If I can help one in distress,*
> *If I can make a burden less,*
> *If I can spread more happiness,*
> *Dear God, may I do it! Amen*
> *(Adapted from "My Daily Prayer"*
> *by Grenville Kleiser)*

# About Being Kind?

2 Samuel 9:1-7
Proverbs 14:21; 19:17
Isaiah 35:3, 4
Micah 6:8
Matthew 4:23; 5:7;9:35-38; 19:20-28; 25:34-40
Mark 9:33-35; 10:35-45
Luke 10:25-37
Galatians 6:9, 10
Philippians 4:14-16
Hebrews 12:12-15

# More to Think About

## Count That Day Lost

If you sit down at set of sun
And count the acts that you have done,
   And, counting, find
One self-denying deed, one word
That eased the heart of him who heard,
   One glance most kind
That fell like sunshine where it went—
Then you may count that day well spent.

But if, through all the livelong day,
You've cheered no heart, by yea or nay—
   If, through it all
You've nothing done that you can trace
That brought the sunshine to one face—
   No act most small
That helped some soul and nothing cost—
Then count that day as worse than lost.

George Eliot

# When Life Is Done

I'd like to think when life is done
That I had filled a needed post.
That here and there I'd paid my fare
With more than idle talk and boast;
That I had taken gifts divine,
The breath of life and manhood fine,
And tried to use them now and then
In service for my fellow men.

Edgar A. Guest

# The House By the Side Of The Road

Let me live in my house by the side of the road,
    Where the race of men go by—
They are good, they are bad, they are weak,
they are strong,
    Wise, foolish—so am I.
Then why should I sit in the scorner's seat
    Or hurl the cynic's ban?—
Let me live in my house by the side of the road
    And be a friend to man.

Sam Walter Foss

# The Parable of
# The
# "Sleeping" Alligator

"Curiosity killed the cat." Have you ever heard someone say that? What does the saying mean? Whose cat was it and what was it doing when it got killed?

Was it in a hen house, in the act of stealing a chicken when a farmer shot it? Or was it away up in a tree about to rob a bird's nest when it fell out of the tree and broke its neck? Or was it a city cat, curious about what was on the other side of the street, who was run over by an automobile when it tried to cross against a red light?

Frankly, I have no answer to these questions, but I do have a story about two little animals who almost lost their lives because of their curiosity. Or was it because of their dis-

78

*obedience? Or did curiosity and disobedience both have something to do with their frightening experience and narrow escape? Figure out the answers for yourself as you hear the story.*

✳ ✳ ✳ ✳ ✳

The animals on Marsh Island were very upset—and no wonder! Bozo Alligator had moved into the lagoon on their nature preserve, and he was anything but welcome! All of the animals were afraid of him and wanted to get rid of him, but what could they do?

Bozo was more than ten feet long, and his body was covered with thick, rough scales that protected him from harm. He had a huge mouth with two rows of sharp teeth, and he ate, not only fish and frogs, but any animals and birds that he could catch! Once the animals sized up the situation, they knew there was no way to get rid of him. "There is only one thing to do," they said to one another, "stay away from the lagoon!" And *that* is what all animals did—that is, all except two!

Who were the two who didn't stay away? Frisky Squirrel and Bunny Rabbit!

One afternoon, as Frisky and Bunny hopped home from school, Bunny said, "Let's take the path that goes by the lagoon; I'd like to see what an alligator looks like."

"So would I," said Frisky, "but we've been warned not to go near the lagoon."

"Phooey!" said Bunny. "I get so tired of parents and teachers saying 'don't-do-this' and 'don't-do-that'!"

"So do I," said Frisky. "And how do they know alligators are dangerous when they have never seen one?"

By this time they were almost to the lagoon.

Just in front of them was a sign in big letters,
"D A N G E R !
NO ANIMALS ALLOWED
BEYOND THIS POINT!"

But Frisky and Bunny didn't even see the words, because just beyond the sign, lying on the bank of the lagoon, was what they came to see—Bozo Alligator!

"Look," whispered Frisky, "there he is! And I believe he is asleep."

"He sure is," Bunny whispered back, as they both moved closer to get a better look at Bozo's head. "Both his eyes are closed tight."

But the truth was that Bozo was only pretending to be asleep. Peeping through the not-quite-closed lid of one eye, Bozo was watching Frisky's and Bunny's every move, and his mouth began to water (or whatever it is that happens to alligators when they begin to feel hungry). He thought, *What a delicious meal; a rabbit and a squirrel! Just right for my dinner!*

In the meantime, Bunny and Frisky were slipping in for a closer look.

We better move away from his head," said Frisky. "Our science teacher warned us that alligators have big mouths and very sharp teeth."

So they moved back close to Bozo's tail and started to count the scales on his back, still thinking he was sound asleep.

And then it happened!

"Now is the time!" Bozo said to himself as he raised his head and looked back. Then, with two flips of his tail, one for Frisky, and one for Bunny, he knocked them both into the middle of the lagoon! Quick as a flash he dived in and started swimming after them. Frisky and Bunny were swimming franticly, trying to reach the other side of the lagoon where they could

climb out and run. But when it came to swimming, they were no match for Bozo. With his mouth open wide, he was gaining on them! He was just about to catch them when a big, brave bird came to their rescue—none other than Mr. Pelican!

He had been standing knee-deep in water on the other side of the lagoon, hoping to catch a fish, and he saw what had happened. In a flash he was in the air. Flapping his strong, wide wings, he flew over to where Bunny and Frisky were swimming with all their might.

Hovering over them for a second, he turned his angry eyes on Bozo. "You cruel monster!" he squawked. "How dare you? You let those dear little animals alone!"

"Mind your own business!" Bozo snarled back. "I'm hungry and am going to get my dinner!"

"That's what you think!" said Mr. Pelican. With wings still flapping, he lowered himself as if he were a helicopter to a point just above the water. Then, with the claw of one foot, he grasped the fur behind the neck of Frisky, and took hold of Bunny in the same way with his other foot. Then, flapping his wings with all his might, he slowly but surely lifted them up out of the water! A moment later, he gently set them down in a bed of leaves at the base of the warning sign they had failed to heed a few minutes earlier.

Mr. Pelican waited until they had blown and sneezed the water out of their noses, then said, "What in the world were you two little animals doing over here at this lagoon? Didn't you hear about Bozo and how dangerous he is? Didn't your parents and teachers warn you to stay away from the lagoon? Didn't you see this sign that says, 'Danger! No Animals Allowed Beyond This Point'"

Frisky looked at Bunny and Bunny looked at Frisky, but both felt so guilty that neither spoke a word!

With that, Mr. Pelican flew back to his fishing, and Frisky and Bunny, after looking once more at the warning sign beside them, started for home. They had learned a lesson they could never forget. Too bad they had to learn it the hard way! And what was that lesson? "Experience is a costly school, but fools will learn in no other!"

\* \* \* \* \*

# Prayer

*Dear God,*
*We thank You for those who want us to grow up safe, sound, and strong, who care enough about us to teach us right from wrong. May we care enough to listen to what they say, and to follow their good advice, day after day. Amen.*

## What Does the Bible Say ...
# About Taking Risks?

Psalm 119:9-11
Proverbs 1:8-10; 3:1, 2; 4:1-5, 10-12; 10:1
Matthew 4:5-11; 6:13,
Luke 6:46-49
Romans 12:21
Ephesians 6:1, 2, 10, 11
James 1:13-15

# More to Think About

## Yield Not

Yield not to temptation,
  For yielding is sin,
Each victory will help you
  Some other to win.
Ask the Savior to help you,
Comfort, strengthen, and keep you,
He is willing to aid you,
He will carry you through.
Horatio R. Palmer

84

# I Will Not Give In

I want to give in,
But I will not give in!
I never will yield!
What, lie down on the field,
And surrender my shield?
No! I will not give in!

I want to give in,
But I will not give in!
Be this ever my song
'Gainst those who go wrong,
O God, make me strong,
That I may not give in!
              (Author unknown)

# The Parable of
# The Lost Eaglet

*How good you are at counting? Let me hear you count yourself—how many of you are there? Just one? Are you sure?*

*Do you sometimes talk to yourself? When you do, how many does that make? At least two, doesn't it? The "you" that does the talking and the "you" that listens and maybe answers. But which of the two is the real you?*

*Perhaps the story that follows will help you find the answer.*

\* \* \* \* \*

From his nest, away up high near the top of a tall pine tree in the forest, the only thing little Baldy Eagle could see was the sky. One morning, when he was still an eaglet only two weeks old, Papa and Mama Eagle were away hunting a mouse for his breakfast, and Baldy began to wonder what the world was like down below. He stepped out to the edge of his nest and looked down. Oh! The world looked wonderful! Baldy leaned forward to get a better view, and whoops! He fell from the edge of the nest and through the branches of the tall pine tree. He flapped his little wings and tried to clutch the branches with his tiny claws, but still he fell—all the way to the bed of pine needles on the ground!

He wasn't hurt, but he was really frightened! What if a wolf or a fox should come along?

But, fortunately for Baldy, it was a young human—who happened to be an eagle scout—who found him. The scout, who lived on a farm, took Baldy home with him, kept him in his house for a few days, and fed him. When he thought Baldy was strong enough, he put him out in the barnyard where there were chickens, turkeys, ducks, and geese.

These barnyard birds had never seen a little eagle before and didn't know what to make of him.

"Let's hear you crow," said Bantam Rooster, who had just learned how to crow himself.

"What do you mean by 'crow'?" Baldy asked.

"I'll show you," Bantam said. He lifted his head, puffed out his chest, and crowed, "Cock-a-doodle-doo!"

Then Baldy tried, but all he could come up with was, "Awk, awk, awk!"

With that, all the chickens cackled, and from that time on they called him "Awk"!

Mr. Turkey was downright cruel. One day he walked over to Baldy and said, "Gobble, gobble, gobble! I don't know what kind of egg you were hatched from, but you really are a strange looking bird. You may be some kind of buzzard, but you are certainly not a turkey! I don't want you scratching in the yard or playing around with our chicks. So stay away from us turkeys or I'll gobble, gobble you up!"

88

Mr. Harry Duck tried to be kind. "Come with me down to the lake," he said. "I'll teach you how to swim."

But once there, he looked at Baldy's feet and said, "Quack, quack! You don't have any webs between your toes! You can't swim!"

Hearing that, Mrs. Owl, who was sitting in a tree close by, said to Baldy: "Hoo, hoo, hoo! Hoo are you anyway?"

That was what troubled Baldy most of all. He didn't know who or what he was. But as time passed, he came to feel more and more that he did not belong in the barnyard! There was one thing about him that was very different from all the other birds in the barnyard; he had great wide wings, and they were growing stronger all the while. How he loved to stretch them—which, of course, made them wider as well as stronger!

The chickens, turkeys, ducks, and geese had wings, too. But they hardly ever stretched them. They just waddled around with their wings folded against their sides, almost as if they had no wings at all. But Baldy kept stretching his, several times every day!

And sometimes as he did, a little voice deep down inside of him seemed to say, "Baldy, you were not made to live in a barnyard. This is not the real you! Your wide wings were given to you for a higher purpose than to be a barnyard fowl. One of these days you will find out who you really are!"

And sure enough, he did!

One day, as he was standing alone by the lake, stretching his wings, he saw a shadow skim across the water. Then he heard a voice—this time not a quiet voice inside him, but a screaming cry up above him!

90

It was Papa Eagle who had found his lost son and was calling to him to come up and fly!

So he did! Baldy stretched out his wings again, then began to flap them. At first slowly, then faster and faster as he found himself rising up and up toward the sky. In the meantime, Papa Eagle was sailing down toward him. By the time they met, Baldy was very tired. He felt he couldn't flap his wings even one more time, and realized he was falling instead of rising.

Then suddenly he felt something solid under his feet, and knew he wasn't falling anymore!

Guess what had happened? Papa Eagle had swooped down under him and was carrying him on his back!

"Baldy," he said, "you were working too hard! When you are up in the air, you don't have to flap your wings. You just need to spread them out, as I am doing now, and the wind currents will carry you! It's what we call soaring!"

"I see," said Baldy, as he slipped off Papa Eagle's back and began soaring beside him.

That was Baldy's first lesson in flying, and before the day was over, Papa Eagle had taught him many others—such as how to dive, how to glide, and how to hover in the air.

Later, the two eagles played hide-and-seek in and out of the floating clouds, then soared over the highest trees on a nearby mountain and back again. Once they dived all the way down to a beautiful meadow where they saw a sparkling river tumbling over rocks.

How happy they were to be together again, and what fun they had!

Then finally, home they sailed to be welcomed by Mama Eagle, who had dinner ready and waiting and was as glad to see Baldy as Papa Eagle had been.

That night, as they were about to go to sleep on a rocky ledge way up on the side of a mountain, Baldy said, "I wonder what that light is away down there in the valley."

"That, said Papa Eagle, "is the farm house near the barnyard where I found you. Want to go back?"

And with that all three gurgled, "Awk, awk, awk," or whatever it is eagles say when they are "happy as larks!"

But which of the three do you suppose was the happiest? I am sure it was Baldy—because you see, he had found his real self! Now he knew who he was and why he had been given his great wide wings!

\* \* \* \* \*

# Prayer

*Dear God,*

*We thank You for that quiet voice inside of us that won't let us be satisfied with what we already are. Also we thank You for our hopes, dreams and ideals that keep us from becoming satisfied with anything but the highest and the best.*

*May we use our high ideals, plus faith and prayer, to become what You want us to be, and to fulfill Your highest purpose for our lives.*

*Each day, while young, strong, and free,*

*May we strive to be the best that we can be.*

*For truth, honor, goodness, and for Thee.*
*Amen.*

## What Does the Bible Say ...
## About Being All You Can Be?

Genesis 37:5-11; 41:38-43
Joshua 1:7-9
1 Chronicles 22:6-16
Psalm 119:9-11
Matthew 5:48; 19:16-22; 25:14-30
Luke 2:52
John 10:10
Romans 12:1-21
Philippians 3:12-16; 4:8
2 Timothy 2:15, 22; 4:7
2 Peter 1:3-11

# More to Think About

## Myself

I have to live with myself, and so
  I want to be fit for myself to know;
I want to be able as days go by
  To look myself straight in the eye....

I don't want to look at myself and know
  That I'm bluster and bluff and empty show.
I never can hide myself from me;
  I see what others may never see;
I know what others may never know;
  I never can fool myself, and so,
Whatever happens, I want to be
  Self-respecting, and conscience-free.

Guest

## I Would Be True

I would be true,
  for there are those who trust me;
  I would be pure, for there are those who care;
I would be strong, for there is much to suffer;
  I would be brave, for there is much to dare.

Howard Arnold Walter

# The Parable of
# The Perky Caterpillar
## (Easter)

*Which would you rather be, if you had to make a choice—a caterpillar or a worm? I would choose to be a caterpillar. A worm keeps on being a worm, as long as it lives, but a caterpillar is able to become a new creature, a creature ever so much more lovely than a caterpillar.*

*This change is so amazing that it might be called a miracle. And the Bible teaches that God is able to work a similar miracle in the life of every one of us, if we will let Him.*

*The story that follows will help you to understand this, and may lead you to want God to change you as He does the caterpillar.*

\* \* \* \* \*

"You are out of your mind!" said Grubby to Perky. Grubby was an earthworm, Perky, a caterpillar. "You are just a worm like me, and no worm can ever fly!"

"But I am not a worm!" replied Perky. "I am a caterpillar, and one day I am going to have wings and fly like a bird."

"You're crazy in the head!" Grubby shot back. "Your name should be Looney, not Perky!" And with that he crawled back into his dark hole in the ground, curled up, and went to sleep.

But, from the green leaf of the milkweed
where he was eating his breakfast, Perky kept
watching the birds, flying from tree to tree singing their happy songs, and the bees flitting from
flower to flower feasting on nectar.

"If I only had wings and could fly like they
do!" he said to himself. Looking up to the blue
sky and back to his clumsy feet, he sighed,
"And if I only knew what I could do to make my
dream come true!"

Just at that moment, the most beautiful creature Perky had ever seen flew down from the
sky and landed on the milkweed leaf right in
front of him.

"Good morning, Perky," said the beautiful
creature.

Perky was so startled he had trouble finding his voice. "Who—who are you—and how did you know my name?" he finally said.

"I am a monarch butterfly, and I am your mother," the beautiful creature answered.

"But you couldn't be my mother," said Perky. "Your face is beautiful, but I have horns in my head and buck teeth! And you have four gorgeous wings, but I have no wings at all—only these clumsy feet!"

"But I am your mother," said the beautiful creature. "My, how you have grown since the day I placed you, a tiny little egg, under a leaf of the milkweed! I heard what you said to Grubby the earthworm. You really want to fly, don't you, Perky?"

"More than anything else in the world!" replied Perky. "But what can I do? Grubby says I'm crazy in the head."

"Grubby is wrong," his mother answered. "Listen while I tell you what to do!

"First, never lose faith, Perky. Keep looking up to the sky, dreaming, hoping and believing with all your heart! Then one of these days you will feel yourself becoming very tired. When that happens, crawl out on a limb of a tree. Then pull out that little spinning wheel from under your chin and spin enough silk to fasten your body firmly to the limb. Your body will then create a chrysalis for you to rest in. Then, all you need to do is curl up, go to sleep, and leave the rest to the warm sun. Now I must be going. Don't forget to do as I have told you."

One afternoon, a few days later, Perky did begin to feel sleepy, and he did exactly what his mother had told him to do. Once he had securely fastened himself to the limb of a tree. Perky began to shed his skin. He had already

97

done this several times in his life, always growing new skin when he had outgrown the old. But this time was different. Instead of growing new skin, a hard shell began to form over Perky, and soon he was covered in a beautiful, shiny chrysalis. Then Perky fell fast asleep.

His bed was so cozy and warm that he slept on and on, day after day, fourteen days altogether. He was so still under his blanket, that he seemed to be dead. But he wasn't! At the end of two weeks he began to stir. As he yawned and stretched, he felt his blanket was too tight. Also he wanted some fresh air.

So he pushed a door through his blanket and stepped out onto the limb above him. And what do you suppose was the first thing he saw?

"Good morning, Perky!"

This time he didn't need to ask who she was.

"Good morning, Mother!" he answered. Then looking around he said, "Oh, Mother, the world is so much more beautiful than ever before!"

"That's because you are looking at it through two new eyes, my son, much stronger than the eyes you had when you were a caterpillar."

Surprised, Perky felt his own head. "And my buck teeth are gone!"

"Yes, and in their place you have a long, slender tongue. With it you will be able to reach far down into the blossom of a flower and suck up nectar to your heart's content. But Perky, you haven't looked behind you to see what is on your back!"

Turning his head, Perky saw four gorgeous wings. "Oh, Mother," he exclaimed, "they're just like yours!"

"Yes, of course," she said, "but they're still wet. You need to move them up and down and let the warm sunshine dry them."

Just then Perky thought about Grubby. "You know, Mother, if Grubby could see me now, he wouldn't call me 'Looney!'"

"Of course not, Perky. Your name is just right for you! *Perky* means full of life!"

"That's just the way I feel, Mother," he said, moving his wings up and down faster and faster.

"I think they are dry now, Perky. Spread them out and let's go!"

Then, side by side, they flew away to explore God's great, beautiful world and to feast on nectar for the rest of their lives!

\* \* \* \* \*

# Prayer

*Dear God,*

*May we never be satisfied with the good when we could do better, and never with the better when we have not yet done our best. Do inspire us with noble dreams, then help us to do our part to make them come true.*

*Just as I am, Thine own to be,*
*Friend of the young, who lovest me,*
*To consecrate myself to Thee,*
*O Jesus Christ, I come.*

*I would live ever in the light;*
*I would work ever for the right;*
*I would serve Thee with all my might;*
*Therefore, to Thee I come.*

*Just as I am, young, strong, and free*
*To be the best that I can be*
*For truth, and righteousness, and Thee,*
*Lord of my life, I come.\* Amen.*

*\*"Just As I am," by Marianne Hearn*

**What Does the Bible Say ...**
# About Becoming New?

Ezekiel 36:26, 27
Luke 15:11-24; 19:1-10
John 1:42; 3:3-8
Acts 22:6-16
Romans 12:2
1 Corinthians 15:35-49
2 Corinthians 3:18; 5:17
Ephesians 2:4-6
Colossians 3:9, 10
1 John 3:2

# More to Think About
## Be Your Best

If you can't be a pine on the top of the hill,
Be a scrub in the valley—but be
The best little scrub by the side of the rill;
Be a bush if you can't be a tree.
If you can't be a highway, then just be a trail,
If you can't be the sun, be a star;
It isn't by size that you win or you fail—
Be the best of whatever you are.

Malloch (adapted)

## The Butterfly

I hold you at last in my hand,
   Exquisite child of the air.
Can I ever understand
   How you grew to be so fair?

You came to my linden tree
   To taste its delicious sweet,
I sitting here in the shadow and shine
   Playing around its feet.

Now I hold you fast in my hand,
    You marvelous butterfly,
Till you help me to understand
    The eternal mystery.

From that creeping thing in the dust
    To this shining bliss in the blue!
God give me courage to trust
    I can break my chrysalis too!
                        Alice Freeman Palmer

## A Youth's Prayer

God, who touches earth with beauty,
    Make me lovely too;
With Thy Spirit re-create me,
    Make my heart anew.

Like Thy springs and running waters,
    Make me crystal pure;
Like Thy rocks of towering grandeur,
    Make me strong and sure.

Like Thy dancing waves in sunlight,
    Make me glad and free;
Like the straightness of the pine trees
    Let me upright be.

Like the arching of the heavens,
    Lift my thoughts above;
Turn my dreams to noble action—
    Ministries of love.

God, who touches earth with beauty,
    Make me lovely too;
Keep me ever, by Thy Spirit,
    Pure and strong and true.
                        Mary S. Edgar

# The Parable of
# The Singing Dove
## (Christmas)

*Among other things, Christmas is the time for giving and receiving gifts. When and how did this tradition start? It began many, many years ago when God gave His Son to be our Savior. His name, as you remember, was Jesus, which means "Savior," and He came as a little baby born in a stable.*

*Had you been there, what would you have given Him for a present on His birthday?*

*This story is about a little dove and the answer he found for that question.*

\* \* \* \* \*

Many, many years ago, in the town of Bethlehem in the country of Palestine, there were some inns where weary travelers could rent rooms in which they could sleep for the night. Behind one of these inns was a stable, and up in a corner under the roof was a little dove whose name was Davey. The stable was his roosting place every night, and usually he had no trouble at all going to sleep. But on one particular night, he found that going to sleep and staying asleep was not easy.

Davey had just said "good-night" to the world, closed his eyes, and tucked his head under his wing, when the innkeeper led a man and his wife into the stable. Davey perked up on his faraway rafter. What were humans doing *here* he wondered at this time of night?

103

The owner of the inn was carrying a lamp and a pitcher of water. He addressed the couple as Joseph and Mary, and said that he was sorry his inn was full, and that he had no other place for them to spend the night. Joseph assured him that they understood. "My wife is very tired, he said. "If you will please leave the lamp and water with us, we will be fine."

Davey watched the man as he carefully prepared a bed of straw for his wife. He tried to make her comfortable, but this was difficult since she was about to give birth to a baby.

Davey strutted anxiously back and forth across his rafter. What if the baby should come *tonight*—here in this shabby, old barn?

When the man and woman were quiet and settled, Davey tucked his head under his wing and settled down a second time. But before long, he was awakened again—this time by the cry of a little baby! "Oh!" cooed Davey to himself. "The baby *has* been born! And I slept right through it!" For quite a while, the man and his wife were busy taking care of the newborn little one. It must have been two hours before Davey, once more, dropped off to sleep.

But before long a group of shepherds arrived at the stable! "What's going on here?" Davey sputtered. "Can't a bird get any sleep tonight?" But thoughts of sleep quickly fled from Davey's mind as he listened to the shepherds tell an amazing story about a message they had received from a band of angels! The angels had appeared in the sky, so the shepherds said, announcing "Glory to God in the highest and on earth peace, goodwill to men." One angel had told them to come to the stable to worship this new baby because He would one day grow up to be the Savior of the world!

The shepherds gazed with loving adoration at the baby, and said wonderful things about Him. Finally, they left. Once more there was quiet, but instead of being sleepy, Davey was wide awake with wonder! Three times he had dropped off to sleep, and three times he had been awakened! But Davey felt he was the most fortunate bird in all the world to be where he was on this particular night. He realized the baby was a very special baby, and he wished he had a gift for Him. But what could he give?

He thought about a feather, but his feathers were not beautiful as were those of the cardinal, the bluebird, or the painted bunting!

He thought of a flower, but there were no flowers in the stable, and in the outside darkness he would not be able to find one.

He thought of singing to the baby, but he did not have a melodious voice such as the Meadowlark, the Mockingbird, or the Nightingale. When Davey did try to sing, all that came out was, "Coo, coo".

Then, within his heart he heard a little voice, "Give to the baby what you have, Davey. That is all God expects and your gift will please both Him and the baby very much!"

By now, Joseph and Mary, both very tired, were fast asleep. The baby had been asleep too, but now He was stirring in the manger! Maybe because there had been so much excitement. Perhaps because the straw in the manger did not make a soft bed such as most babies have waiting for them. Whatever the cause, the baby was beginning to fuss, and Davey feared that He would soon break into loud crying. "Maybe I can keep the baby quiet so Mary and Joseph can continue sleeping," he said to himself. So, he flew down from his roost, perched on the side of

106

the manger and began singing, ever so quietly, the only song he knew and the only words he could say, "Coo, coo, coo."

And do you know what happened? Davey's song was so soft and soothing, that the baby closed His little eyes and was soon sound asleep again.

Joseph and Mary were still sleeping too, but not Davey! He stayed there on the side of the manger waiting to sing his little song again if the Baby stirred and need to be lulled back to sleep.

God was so pleased with what Davey had done, that He did a very wonderful thing! He placed Davey's song into the voicebox of all the babies who have ever been born! To this day, the first word many babies utter is, "Coo, coo, coo."

And how do mothers feel about that? As everyone knows, there's no song in all the world sweeter to a loving mother's ear than the "cooing" of her little baby. Many times a loving mother will respond by holding her baby close to her heart and singing back, "Coo, coo, coo, I love you. Yes, I do, coo, coo, coo."

✳ ✳ ✳ ✳ ✳

# Prayer

## A Christmas Carol

What can I give him,
   Little as I am?
If I were a shepherd,
   I would give him a lamb;
If I were a wise man,
   I would do my part,
But what can I give him?
   I will give him my heart!
               Amen.
     (Christina G. Rossetti,
           adapted.)

**What Does the Bible Say ...**
# About the Birth of Jesus and the Giving of Gifts?

Matthew 1:18-25
Mark 12:41-44
Mark 14:3-9
Luke 2:1-20
John 3:16, 17
2 Corinthians 9:15
Philippians 2:6-8
1 John 4:9-11

108

# More to Think About

## Incarnate Love

Love came down at Christmas,
   Love all lovely, love divine;
Love was born at Christmas,
   Star and angels gave the sign.

Love shall be our token,
   Love be yours and love be mine,
Love to God and all men,
   Love for plea and gift and sign.
                Christina Rossetti

## Away In a Manger

Away in a manger, No crib for a bed,
The little Lord Jesus Laid down His sweet head;
The stars in the sky Looked down where He lay,
The little Lord Jesus, asleep on the hay.

The cattle are lowing, The poor baby wakes,
But little Lord Jesus, No crying he makes;
I love thee, Lord Jesus! Look down from the sky,
And stay by my cradle To watch lullaby.

Be near me, Lord Jesus! I ask Thee to stay
Close by me forever, and love me, I pray;
Bless all the dear children in Thy tender care,
And fit us for heaven, to live with Thee there.

         First two verses by Martin Luther
     Third verse by John Thomas McFarland

# Christmas Prayer

Let not our hearts be busy inns,
  That have no room for Thee,
But cradles for the living Christ
  And His nativity.
      Ralph Spaulding Cushman

## Wise Men Seeking Jesus

Wise men seeking Jesus
  Traveled from afar,
Guided on their journey
  By a beauteous star.
But if we desire Him,
  He is close at hand;
For our native country
  Is our holy land.

He is more than near us,
  If we love Him well;
For He seeketh ever
  In our heart to dwell.
            James East

## A Christmas Prayer

We open here our treasures and our gifts;
And some of it is gold, and some is frankin-
  cense,
And some is myrrh;
For some has come from plenty, some from joy,
And some from deepest sorrow of the soul.
But Thou, O God, dost know the gift is love,
Our pledge of peace, our promise of good-will.
Accept the gift and all the life we bring.
            Herbert H. Hines

# The Shepherds Had an Angel

The shepherds had an angel,
　　The wise men had a star,
But what have I, a little child,
　　To guide me home from far,
Where glad stars sing together,
　　and singing angels are?

Lord Jesus is my Guardian,
　　So I can nothing lack;
The lambs lie in His bosom,
　　Along life's dangerous track;
The willful lambs that go astray,
　　He, bleeding, fetches back.

Christ watches me, His little lamb,
　　Cares for me day and night,
That I may be His own in heaven:
　　So angels clad in white
Shall sing their 'Glory, glory,'
　　For my sake in the height.
　　　　　Christina Georgina Rossetti


# How Far to Bethlehem?

It isn't far to Bethlehem town!
It's anywhere that Christ comes down
And finds in people's friendly faces
A welcome and abiding place.
The road to Bethlehem runs right through
The homes of folks like me and you.
　　　　　Madeleine Sweeny Miller